21 Ways To Find (
Proven Marketing Strateg *es To Finding Lucrative De*
By Jeff Leighton

M000100267

Text copyright © 2016 Jeff Leighton
All Rights Reserved

Table of Contents

Introduction

Hey, I want to thank you for downloading this book, **21 Ways To Find Off Market Real Estate: Proven Marketing Strategies To Finding Lucrative Deals**.

Over the last 5 years I have dedicated myself to learning and mastering the off market real estate world. During that time, I've done numerous deals, worked with some of the top deal makers in the country, and seen firsthand the amazing profit potential of off market properties, including making $35,000 on my very first off market deal.

I've now been fortunate to teach other investors and deal hunters across the country on how to consistently find these off market opportunities that I share in this book.

I will say that I did not get to where I am in the off market world overnight. I have spent countless hours studying marketing, real estate, going to seminars, paying tens of thousands of dollars for mentors, and experimenting with as many marketing strategies as you can think of to gain a consistency in this business.

A lot of what I tried did not work and I wasted tons of time and money but gained experience from the process and came out stronger as a result. Everything that even showed a promise of hope of working I scaled up and stuck with and have now applied many of these tactics to my off market business.

The result? I get more off market real estate leads each and every week than I ever thought possible and my off market business continues to grow.

I am now going to give you all of these marketing strategies that I have applied and used to find some of the white hot deals that you would not even think exist. I have actually compiled a list of the 21 top strategies for finding these deals, many of which I have tested and have worked for me.

Are all of these strategies and ideas going to work for you? Maybe, maybe not, but either way I would strongly encourage you to try as many as you can, take massive action, and stick with what works.

Some of these marketing tactics are capable of dramatically changing your life since just one off market deal can drastically increase your income, much less if you did 3, 5, 10, or even 30 in one year. Once you consistently learn how to generate these leads then nobody can take that skill from you and in ANY economy you will be able to generate consistent discounted properties that you can buy, sell, or joint venture on.

This is the best of what has worked in my business and with the top investors that I work with. I invite you to try these strategies out and learn from my successes, failures, and experiences.

My goal is that you save a lot of time, money, and headache by trying what actually works which is all below. Enjoy and once you do your first couple of off market deals, send me a testimonial!

Before We Get Started…

I want to be very clear as I feel that this is often overlooked.

You can have the very best marketing strategies in the world HOWEVER, if you do not implement these tactics you will get zero results, I can assure you of that.

If you do not consistently put out marketing then you will not get any leads and no leads equals no deals. Think of leads as the lifeline of your business. I see myself as a marketing business more so than a real estate business because I am always marketing.

You can read this as many times as you want but the person that reads just one paragraph and actually implements a strategy is going to be light years ahead of the non-action taker.

Keep in mind, these strategies all work however they are going to work differently depending on the market you are in. I would recommend you research your market as much as possible and you can start with local articles on real estate, attending REIA events, talking with other investors, and getting a feel for what type of market you are in and what strategies people like to use.

Another point to keep in mind is you need to think of your marketing as a system. You need to create some type of system around your marketing efforts, it can't just be you doing things here and there, there has to be consistency and output. Think of ways that you could contact at least 1000 people every single month because that is when you will start to see results by taking mass action. If you are contacting just 25 people every week or month you should not expect to see much results. Some of the top investors I know will even contact up to 10,000 of the right people a month about selling their house after qualifying them by various criteria.

NOTE: All of these strategies work when implemented properly however like any marketing strategy you will get people here and there that will tell you they are not interested. Don't get discouraged by anyone that tells you to stop contacting them or to take them off the list. When I first got started I LOVED it when anyone would respond to my marketing because I knew all it took was 50 leads to find the 1 that was a good deal. Be steady in your marketing and reap the rewards.

Now that we got all that out of the way, let's jump into actual strategies you can use today to find these great off market deals.

Pro Tips For Finding Wholesalers And Bird Dogs

Working with wholesalers and bird dogs is an effective free strategy that countless investors use to find consistent deals. Wholesalers and bird dogs are people who do the dirty work of finding off-market deals. Essentially, they can serve you the deal on a silver platter. Most of the time, they are newer investors who do the marketing and legwork to find deals for off-market investors with the necessary funds and experience.

By doing a lot of networking and online research you can find out who the local wholesalers and/or bird dogs in your area are. REIA meetings and Meetup groups are a great place to find those types of investors. You can also search wholesalers on LinkedIn for your area; if you live in a big city, there should be at least 25-50 on there.

Every city has wholesalers, so it's a good idea to build a solid list of wholesalers who can send you deals. Having just a couple of wholesalers will give you some leads. However, if you want to be consistent, you must have a minimum of ten wholesalers in your group – and ideally, 25 or so is even better. Keep in mind the 80/20 rule, which states that 80 percent of the deals will come from 20 percent of the wholesalers. Be sure to find the most active wholesalers and get on their good side. I know some investors who like to wine and dine with their wholesalers, and sometimes even assist with their marketing. You, as the off-market investor, want to be the first person a wholesaler thinks of when they get a great deal under contract.

If you have a list of 25 wholesalers, you can email them once a month, to make sure you are at the top of their mind and you will get consistent leads from them. I know one investor in the area who brags about the assignment fees he pays out, and he makes a killing from just working with wholesalers.

I suggest combining the strategy of working with wholesalers and an additional marketing strategy, such as direct mail or bandit signs. However, I will let you be the judge. Keep in mind that most wholesaler leads will be similar to other types of leads you get, which means they won't be the greatest. However, out of ten wholesaler leads, there should be at least one very good, if not great, deal. You just have to be patient and let your wholesaler know exactly what your standards are so that they don't just send over anything.

The great thing about this type of lead is that it is free. If you buy one from a wholesaler or bird dog, they will typically work even harder to find you deals. Being a wholesaler or bird dog for a more experienced investor is a great way to get started in the real estate investment and off-market business.

YouTube Domination

YouTube is a medium that has been growing in popularity and is now one of the top online places to market your business. It is easy (and quite fun) to set up a channel and create videos, many of which can be made on your iPhone. There are also plenty of free video editing services that can help you make professional-looking videos, such as Video Pad.

If you want to set up your channel to look professional, you can go to Fiverr.com, which has numerous resources available for $5-25, including channel banners. You can even use it to hire professional actors and actresses for short videos if you don't feel like being in the video yourself.

Once you have a YouTube channel, I suggest giving out free information or making short videos on how to sell a house fast. Make sure to target keywords that a potentially motivated seller would type in. It is fairly easy for videos to rank high on YouTube, and sometimes even on the first page of Google. Usually, if you want a website to rank on the first page of Google by means of normal SEO tactics, that could take months. However, the algorithm places a lot more importance on video and, as a result, you can rank a YouTube video for "we buy houses in (insert your city here)" fairly quickly and easily.

I know many investors and off-market specialists that have grown their channel immensely over the last couple years. They do not only use their videos to find off-market deals, but also to connect with other investors and joint venture partners, and to get free publicity for their business. I have several videos that rank extremely high – some are even on the first page of Google for those keywords. I would recommend browsing around on other real estate investors' YouTube channels, as well as other popular channels across YouTube, to get ideas for your own.

If you want to do paid ads on YouTube, then those are fairly easy to set up, as well as shockingly inexpensive. Usually, you can run paid video ads before a YouTube video for as little as 5 cents per view. This could get you in front of thousands of people for a minimal amount of money. Some people in related industries focus their marketing on YouTube and get hundreds of thousands of views.

Make sure that your YouTube ads are running in front of potentially motivated sellers, and not just the general public. Targeted YouTube ads are very similar to AdWords or pay-per-click. Basically, you can select certain keywords to make sure that your ad is only running in front of people who typed in your keywords. You can also do retargeting with your YouTube ads so that only people who have visited your site in the past get to see them. We will go more into retargeting and pay-per-click in another section, but this is just a heads-up.

Another great thing about YouTube is that once you get good at it, other real estate professionals, and sometimes even other businesses, will start contacting you about doing videos (and paying you) since most people don't know the best practices on YouTube.

Perfectly Legal Search Engine Optimization (SEO) Tips

Whether you are looking for off-market properties or other opportunities, SEO (search engine optimization) should be a part of your marketing plan, since everyone is online these days. SEO is what you do to make your websites organically rank high on Google and other search engines. It is a combination of including keywords and optimizing parts of your pages, as well as adding valuable content that users find engaging.

Since the overwhelming majority of real estate searches begins online, SEO must be a part of your strategy. Google tracks nearly everything and is always improving its algorithm – so when you optimize a blog post or website for a keyword, keep in mind that you also need to provide good content. Google is always cracking down on people who spam by writing the keyword 100 times throughout their page (this is an extreme example, but it happens).

My recommendation for ranking high for specific keywords is to look at what similar businesses in other states or cities are doing to rank on the first page, and then emulate those. There are also freely available lists of the top keywords that real estate investors should use for their SEO. For example, you could look at the companies that rank high for "sell house fast Phoenix" or different areas, and use that as a blueprint for your own SEO. I have learned a ton about search engine optimization from modeling other investment companies.

Since SEO tactics do not have immediate results like some other strategies, such as direct mail, bandit signs, or pay-per-click, I would recommend incorporating SEO into your overall marketing plan without making it your #1 strategy. SEO should be a complementary marketing strategy and is more of an effective long-term tactic for marketing. There are plenty of free resources online for learning how to rank high with different websites, videos, photos, and more. Since SEO is free (unless you pay a consultant), I suggest including this strategy in your overall marketing plan.

Powerful Joint Ventures

Joint ventures will open up a whole new range of deal flow possibilities for you. If you'd like to go more into detail, you can check out the amazing marketing strategist named Jay Abraham, who has entire books and seminars on joint venture partnerships. I will go over a couple of ways I have seen joint ventures work out.

When I first got started in the off-market world, I had a scarcity mindset: I didn't want to work with or assist my so-called competition, not in a million years. However, that soon changed after I partnered with a couple of wholesalers on deals and learned that win-win joint ventures are everywhere if you know how to look for them. You can always tell a newer investor from an experienced one; the newer one will typically want nothing to do with their competition, while the top-of-the-market investors embrace competition and think of ways to work together so that everyone can do more deals.

The key to successful joint ventures is that if there is any red flag that gives you an uneasy feeling, you should refrain from joint venturing. I remember that one real estate agent I worked with told me he went to law school because he gets sued a lot. That was about as big of a red flag as there could be. However, I still decided to work with him. Within the first 30 days, I could already see what a nightmare it would be to work with him.

Another red flag I encountered in the business was when my broker considered hiring a person who had been out of work for several years. You should never hire someone who has been out of work for so long, especially in a great economy. The same is true for contractors: You never want to hire a contractor who is not "busy". Not surprisingly, this person lasted only several months before the relationship grew too toxic. You also want to be careful about joint venturing with family and friends until you have a good amount of experience. For your first couple of deals, I would only suggest partnering with people that have a lot of experience. Here are a couple ways to joint venture:

Strategy #1 – If you find a great off-market lead that you don't know what to do with, you can reach out to a trustworthy wholesaler or top home buyer in your area and ask them to send the property out to their list once you get it under contract. I have profitably used this strategy many times and will continue to do so. The key is to find an experienced, trustworthy investor with a large list that can reach many potential buyers. Just make sure you are not breaking any regulations by acting as a real estate agent if you have a license. I would recommend checking with your local real estate attorney or broker. This strategy can open up a whole other profit stream that you miss out on when you don't chase leads you are unsure of.

Strategy #2 – If you find an amazing deal that you want to buy but don't have the money and experience, often your competitors would be willing to lend you the money or even do the complete rehab. You would be surprised at how many times my direct competition has offered different partnerships depending on the deal. Some investors have a ton of cash sitting around but no deals to invest in, while other investors have a ton of leads but not enough cash to buy the homes. Everything is negotiable, and people are always looking for ways to do more deals, whether they are the lender, wholesaler, rehabber, agent, or another type of partner.

Strategy #3 – If you are a real estate agent who finds a great off-market lead, you can bring the deal to one of your investors, have them pay your buyer's agent fee of 3%, and then get the listing on the back end once the property is renovated. This happens all the time, and it can be a great way to get two deals in one. This is also a smart way to market to real estate agents if you are an investor looking for more deals. Let any agent know that if they bring you an off-market deal that you can purchase, they can get both the buyer's side of the commission and the seller's when they go to list it.

The great thing about joint ventures is that there are countless ways to do it. The only limitation on joint ventures is your imagination. When you are first getting started, I recommend you to reach out to or partner with the top buyer in your area until you feel comfortable doing deals by yourself, and then you can go in any direction you want. As an example of the countless ways to work together, I know a company that started their business by wholesaling, which eventually turned into rehabbing, which then turned into rehabbing and coaching others how to flip homes. Now they rehab homes, coach others, and lend money nationwide as hard moneylenders to their students as well as to other investors, many in their own backyard. I imagine that five years from now, they will have evolved even further and added an additional income stream.

Direct Mail Mojo

Direct mail is the most potent strategy for buying houses because it is so targeted. I will explain how it works below. Just like any type of marketing, it needs to be systematized with mass action. Despite all the new social media and changes in technology, I still consider direct mail the #1 source of deals for the top investors I work with across the country.

The first step in direct mail is getting a list of motivated prospects. Getting the right list is 90% of the equation. You should only invest time in sending mail to the right prospects. Some examples of motivated prospects include people who are confronted with pre-foreclosure, probate, eviction, and absentee owners.

The good news is that there are plenty of places where you can get lists. A couple of companies that sell lists include List Source and US Probate Leads. However, if you are savvy enough, you can find much of this data in your courthouse records. I got started by sending out just 20 or 30 letters a week, and now I could send out 5,000 postcards without batting an eye. I even know some off-market specialists that send out up to 10,000 letters every month. It is amazing to me how many people tell me direct mail does not work. When I ask them how many letters they send out each month, their number is usually under 25.

Once you have your list, the second step is to choose a direct mail letter or postcard to mail out. I would recommend going with a proven postcard or yellow letter, of which there are plenty of examples online. If you Google "Richard Roop postcard", you can find some of the best cards freely available. Some investors and real estate agents try to completely change the design and layout. While their new design might work, it is wiser to go with what has proven to work time and time again.

A quick tip on postcards is that fancy designs and beautiful images of homes rarely work. You need to have a lot of text and a call to action if you want to be successful in the direct mail business. Direct mail is not about art, even though most marketing design professionals would probably tell you that you need scenic images and glossy photos. However, if you study direct mail like I have, you will learn that direct mail is almost like having a salesman go to each door you send mail to, and that's why you need to have as much information on the card or letter as possible.

Once you have your list and mail pieces, it's time to send out your first campaign, as well as plan your second, third, and fourth one. The thing with direct mail is that it is only effective after mailing a minimum of three times. If you do not have the patience to mail that many times, then I would not even try this campaign. Most investors or agents will mail once, maybe get a call or two, and then stop mailing. I typically mail five times over the course of six months, and I also have one of the best mailing lists available.

When I first got started, I would track how many phone calls I could get through direct mail. I started with just two or three leads a month and made it my goal to add ten leads each month, until I hit 50 leads in a month. At 50 leads in a month, you start to see a lot of off-market deal possibilities. It is fun, and you can make a competition out of driving leads to your business line. The top company in my area gets up to 500 leads a month from their various sources; however, to be successful you really only need 50 a month. Then, once you see fit, you can scale it up.

Some services that can help you get your mail out include www.click2mail.com, Yellow Letters Complete, and Real Prospect 2009. There are also some great inexpensive books out there on direct mail marketing, including anything by Dan Kennedy. This is a marketing medium that has stayed consistent throughout the rise of social media, and I imagine it will continue to do so. No amount of Instagram posts or tweets can replicate a personalized, physical card in the mail.

Bandit Sign Breakthroughs

Bandit signs are a highly effective and inexpensive strategy of lead generation that you see in nearly every city in America. Bandit signs are the signs saying "we buy houses" that you see when driving around. One sign typically costs about $2, and there are countless places online where you can order them. Some real estate agents and investors scoff at these signs, but I have seen first-hand testimonials from investors who have made six-figure profits off them. The real strategy to bandit signs involves outsourcing the process, mapping out the signs, and verifying that they go up. Let me explain. Every type of marketing needs a system, and the system for bandit signs goes as follows.

1)   Use Google Maps and/or another tool to map out different places for your signs in low to median income areas with lots of investment properties. Once you have about 25 places for your signs to go up, you can move on to step #2. You can also have a real estate agent pull up the hot zip codes where there have been a lot of cash transactions and investment deals. I know some people that even negotiate with shops, gas stations, etc. to put their signs on the property, knowing that thousands of cars drive by.

2)   You should put up signs once a week. The first couple of times, you should probably do it yourself so that you can get an idea of how long the route takes. Once you outsource the process, you will know exactly

how much time it requires, and you can pay someone accordingly.

      3)   You should hire a local to put up 25 signs a week (minimum), with a total of 100 signs a month. You should also have them take a photo of all 25 signs so that you don't have to drive all around town to make sure they are up. I have heard of people hiring someone local, only to find all the signs in the dumpster five hours later.

One of the pitfalls I see with newer investors is that they put up ten signs, get a call or two, and then say that bandit signs don't work. You need to be consistent and get up a bunch of signs.

Always check with your local county ordinances to make sure they are legal in your area, as I have heard of investors getting fined for bandit signs. You should also only use a business phone number on these signs, i.e. you do not want to put your cell phone on there.

Since you are putting up signs for the general public, your calls will not be as targeted as direct mail; however, you will get calls, and usually about one in ten is from a motivated seller. When you are getting started, this is a great, proven marketing strategy that can consistently bring in leads in the areas you are looking to buy. I know some investors that put large signs with a phone number on the houses where they are working. In terms of getting the signs out, you could look to partner with someone putting up signs for another business (furniture, massage, we buy gold, fitness, etc.) and offer to split the cost with them.

Door Hangers and Door Knocking Advice

Door knocking and using door hangers is one of the most old-school and effective campaigns there are. Think of this style of marketing as a political campaign to get the vote out – it is the same idea. In fact, if you want to hire someone, look for people with experience running political campaigns. Often, those jobs are seasonal and don't pay very well, so this could be the perfect part-time or full-time job for them.

Door knocking works exactly the way it sounds: You or your marketing people go door to door, asking locals if they know of anyone looking to sell their home and explaining that you pay a referral fee of $1,000 for any closed sale. Most people will not be home, and if they are, they will most likely not be interested. However, like any type of marketing, this is a numbers game: If you were to knock on 100 doors a day, you would be putting 100 door hangers out and possibly have two or three people with an interest in selling. If you were to knock on just 100 doors every day, that would be 500 door hangers a week, which results in 2,000 a month. You would also be talking with potentially 10-20 motivated sellers every single week, for a total of 40 to 80 every month. These numbers can add up quickly, especially if you decide to contact more than 100 people per day.

This type of strategy can also be outsourced fairly easily to an intern or marketing specialist. All you have to do is give them a route to walk, provide them with a script, and then keep track of who answered and who did not. If you had someone doing this full time, and you just did one deal per month, this strategy could be worth your time. As long as you are in an urban area where you can knock on a lot of doors each day, it can be very effective.

I know development teams that rely almost exclusively on this face-to-face type of strategy. The one off-market specialist who taught me this strategy had to pause their door-knocking campaign because it was so effective that they had their hands full with numerous houses. If you cannot yet afford to hire someone, maybe you could do it in your lunch break for an hour or so. It is good exercise, and also a great way to get to know the neighborhoods and streets.

Pay-Per-Click (PPC) Opportunity

Pay-per-click has become one of the best strategies for consistently sourcing great off-market leads, as well as investors for your deals, and more. One of the great things about pay-per-click is that you can create a campaign and start getting leads the next day. Since you can search by narrow (or broad) keywords, you can target exactly the prospect you are looking for, such as "sell my house fast in Dallas".

One thing I also love about pay-per-click is that you only pay when someone actually clicks on your ad. You are essentially paying for performance (per click), unlike some other types of marketing, where you could send out hundreds of letters or put up signs all over the city, for which you pay a good amount of money, without getting any calls. One thing that every good marketer should understand is how much each lead is costing them. With pay-per-click, it is very easy to measure how many clicks there are, how many conversions you get, what the cost per lead is, and more.

To optimize your PPC (pay-per-click) campaign the first thing you should do is educate yourself on how the AdWords system works. Too many investors and real estate agents just start a campaign without having done any research whatsoever into what makes an effective AdWords campaign. There are plenty of free resources online, as well as inexpensive books on Amazon. For example, I would recommend anything by Perry Marshall. I have three basic tips on setting up an affective AdWords campaign:

1)   Do proper keyword research into exactly what type of person you are looking for, e.g. "sell house fast Dallas". You have to be selective and think about who exactly is typing in these keywords. If there is a one-in-three chance it could be a motivated seller,

then I would include the keyword. Also use negative keywords that eliminate a lot of people searching homes or looking to sell their house with a realtor.

2) Ad groups. With AdWords, using ad groups is absolutely essential to refine your marketing and get only the highest-quality leads. There are numerous free resources online that create ad groups. This is a must if you are doing AdWords.

3) Use AdWords extensions. When you look at all the paid ads from a Google search, you will see some ads that have links to additional information, such as a phone number, FAQs, and more. Those advertisers are using ad extensions to make their ad look more professional, as well as increase its size. Nearly all the top marketers in any industry do this, and you would be wise to do the same.

When in doubt, you should model the top marketers and business people such as Perry Marshall, Tony Robbins, or even large companies like Nike or Whole Foods. By studying and applying just a few core principles of pay-per-click advertising, you can move up the ranks of the skilled marketers doing this type of advertisement. Most of the people that do pay-per-click waste their time and money by not following the basic principles above or the ones that Perry Marshall talks about in his AdWords books. If you have a good-sized marketing budget, you can even outsource the process to an AdWords specialist until you get a good feel for how the process and system work.

Television Ad Tactics

Television ads are a much more advanced and expensive strategy that you should only use once you have established a track record of doing deals. However, it can be one of the best mediums for lead generation because you can get in front of tens of thousands of people.

One company I know absolutely crushes it with TV advertising and has been buying off-market deals for years with this strategy. The brand awareness these ads have created has made them the go-to company in the area. Everybody thinks of them when they have a house in disrepair that they need to sell fast. This type of advertising looks much more professional than a handwritten bandit sign on a street corner.

It is important for you to realize that TV ads will often create a ton of leads in a short period of time, so you need to have some type of system to make sure you answer all the calls and capture all the leads. A tip for creating commercials would be to look around at the "we buy houses" videos on YouTube, find a couple that you like, and incorporate those elements into your TV ad.

Obviously, TV ads are significantly more expensive than any other type of medium, so this strategy is for experts only.

Tap Into Radio Ads

Radio advertising is a more advanced strategy that has proven to be effective for experienced investors with a larger marketing budget. In any city in America, if you listen to the radio long enough, you will hear ads for "we buy houses" from local investment companies. This is a great way to generate leads if you have systems in place to capture all the calls that come in. Usually, with radio ads, the leads will come in quickly and then disappear, so you need to have a person or two who is capable of handling them.

They are obviously less expensive than TV ads and significantly easier to produce, since all you need is a professional recording. One of the great things about radio ads is that it offers another medium for people to see – or in this case, hear – your company, which can build more trust and result in your customers calling you. Another advantage of radio is that it is local so you are not sending out your message to people in different states to whom it would have little relevance.

One downside to radio is that many people listen while driving so it is not always ideal for them to pick up the phone and call you, unless you have a memorable phone number or ad. There are plenty of case studies of successful radio ads available online that you can emulate. Just like with any type of marketing, I would recommend testing this strategy by starting small and scaling up if you see it could have traction.

Dog Walking Nonsense

When I was doing research for additional off-market strategies, I came across one real estate agent who claims to be the off-market real estate "specialist" with thousands of off market homes a month. One of his top strategies for finding deals was talking to dog walkers. I kid you not; that was his strategy. Now, if I were to ask him whether he has actually tried that strategy for finding off-market deals, or whether he or any of his agents have done an off-market deal that way, I am almost certain the answer would be no.

I would love to follow up with this agent and have him tell us more about this dog walking strategy, but my guess is that he probably just talked about it so that he could get his name out there as a so-called off-market expert.

How practical is the dog walking strategy? Maybe you could find all the dog walkers in your neighborhood and ask them to keep their eyes open for off-market properties. Then you could pay them per lead or work out some type of arrangement that works for both parties. It could be worth exploring.

Maybe this so-called off-market expert does have a team of dog walkers that find all his off-market deals for him; I am not sure. I was just a little surprised to see this newer strategy that I had never heard before. As we all know, the media is never wrong, so if they say this agent is the off-market expert, then it must be true (☺).

Stunning Open House Strategy

A friend of mine has an amazing strategy for generating leads, private money, joint venture partners, etc. for his business. I like to call it the open house strategy; however, this tactic is much more strategic than a basic open house on the weekend with purple balloons, free mints, and a sign-in sheet.

This is what he does. For some of the houses he is rehabbing or is about to rehab, he sends out an invitation to his list of buyers for a free one-hour training at the house. During the training, he discusses how he found the deal, how he financed it, and what types of renovations he is going to do. This creates a lot of buzz and brings many people in the real estate investment world to the house to learn more, network, and possibly invest or partner on the next deal.

At the event, people ask plenty of questions, and they often bring friends or associates. When everyone fills in the sign-in sheet, my friend can add new contacts to his database. I first met him at one of these trainings, where I learned how I could work with him on different wholesales and rehabs. Since then, we have partnered on numerous deals and continue to do so today. I am now one of the many testimonials on his website.

By doing these free trainings at pre-renovated and post-renovated homes, he has generated private money lenders, wholesalers, and realtors who bring him more deals and plenty of recognition throughout the area. People see him as the go-to guy if there is a house that needs fixing up, and he gets many off-market deals from this strategy. Since it is such an easy strategy to implement (just email your list), I would recommend any off-market investor to at the very least try it.

He is the only person I have seen who applies this strategy, but I feel that every investor should be doing it. The open house strategy only takes about an hour, yet it can build a whole new group of people that can invest in your deals and send you deals. Moreover, it helps you to build more credibility as an off-market specialist. If you are worried about liability, then only do free trainings at post-renovated houses (instead of pre-renovated homes). Perhaps you could also offer free food and drinks for attendees. This unique form of marketing and promotion can be a lot of fun and provide a change of pace.

(☆) Do Something that makes You Stand out (orange Shoes) So ppl remember You

Hidden Secrets of Meetup Groups

Hosting Meetup groups has recently become a popular way to find more deals, more lenders, and more joint venture partners. If you really want to crush it in the off-market world, you *need* to have your own Meetup group.

The Meetup group is similar to the aforementioned open house strategy; however, with Meetup groups you can attract as many as 50 or even 100 people, and the meetings are usually held at hotels or offices. I know one local company that has about 500 active members in their group, including real estate agents, wholesalers, other investors, and lenders. Once a month, this company holds a training where they teach a marketing principle of how to source deals. The idea with this Meetup group is that by training potentially hundreds of people on how to find deals, they now have a whole new source of lead opportunities. These people will most likely come to them with any potential deal they have.

During the meetups, the company explains how people can send them deals and joint venture possibilities, depending on how good of a deal it is. This is a genius strategy that has resulted in numerous opportunities for everyone involved with it. If you go on to Meetup.com for your local area, you can probably find several different types of Meetup groups for real estate investing or off-market real estate. I would recommend going to as many as possible since it allows you to build your team and learn.

Keep an open mind knowing that some Meetup groups are professionally run and some are not. No matter what, you can always learn something new and make new connections. You can even take notes on what you like or dislike about each meetup group you attend so that when you create your own, you will know exactly what to do.

Call Fire Revelation and Cold Calling

Cold calling is an old-school, effective way of digging up lucrative leads in any market. Many agents and investors use cold calling effectively. Now, there is a "do not call" list, so use this strategy at your own risk.

The most popular service I have heard of for cold calling is CallFire, with which you can ask literally tens of thousands of people each month if they are looking to sell their house. In the world of cold calling, at least half of the people will not answer. So let's say you use the CallFire service and call 20,000 people in one month, which is realistic. Out of those 20,000, at least 10,000 will not answer. Out of the 10,000 that do reply, probably only 1-3% are looking to sell their house. Out of that 1-3%, you should only look for the top leads, since most people are looking for a retail price and would be better off with a real estate agent.

Cold calling is something you could try doing yourself at first; however, I would recommend outsourcing this service. There are plenty of people available on Upwork that can make calls for you. I used to work in the direct sales cold calling business, and I know first-hand how rewarding it can be to find the right prospect, especially if you outsource the entire thing and don't have to do any work for it!

The White Pages or any other type of listing service is a very inexpensive way of generating leads. Remember that the off-market business, like most businesses, is about generating leads above all else. If you can get this part down, you have the majority of the business down.

Maximize Real Estate Agents

Working with real estate agents is a rather obvious strategy for finding off-market deals; however, most people are not strategic about this. They might work with one or two agents, but they don't really know how to build a team of agents that scour the city looking for deals. Before I go into this killer strategy, keep in mind that most agents do not work with off-market real estate or investors. Some may not have any interest in finding those types of deals.

I learned this strategy from a friend who worked for a very successful off-market investor in the area. One of their marketing tactics was contacting every single real estate agent who had done a deal in the last six months. They let these agents know that if they came across a fixer upper deal, they wanted to know about it, and they would give them the buyer's agent commission and let them list the property once it was renovated.

Of the 500 agents that they reached out to, only about 10 percent were responsive, but out of those they found a solid group of 25 agents that were active in the business and would consistently send them deals. With real estate agents, wholesalers, and other joint venture partners, you have to realize it is going to be a numbers game. When you contact ten agents or wholesalers, you cannot expect all of them to consistently find off-market deals for you. You need to take massive action, and go above and beyond what most people would consider reasonable.

The great thing about this strategy is that it is free – it only costs time, which isn't necessarily a problem if you outsource it to an assistant. Most investors usually only talk to one or two agents, but by reaching out to basically the entire city, you can find the best agents for your team. If you combine this strategy with working with wholesalers, as well as doing another marketing campaign like direct mail, then you will never run out of leads for your business.

Craigslist Ads Jumpstart

Craigslist ads are a good way to generate free leads when you are getting started. Since anyone with a user account can post "we buy houses" or "sell your house fast" ads, it is not hard to start advertising on this medium. This is a good beginner strategy to get your feet wet.

I would never rely on this type of marketing for deals, but if you are consistent in posting different types of ads, then you can typically get consistent leads every single month. You can also see who else is posting ads on "we buy houses" and network with them to see how you can work together. One of my best cash buyers found me on Craigslist, and since then we have done numerous deals together. There are plenty of free templates for real estate ads available online.

You can also look through who is selling their property directly on Craiglist – believe it or not, some people do – and send them an email. By directly contacting sellers who post their property on Craigslist, you will get a much higher response rate than by just posting a "we buy houses" ad.

Since the barrier to entry is so low, you will get a lot of people who may or may not have any idea what they are talking about. You will get some interesting replies to your ads, so keep that in mind.

Discover Mass Texting

Mass texting is a newer strategy that has been gaining a lot of momentum recently. The way mass texting works is exactly how it sounds. If you can gain access to a list of motivated sellers, you can use a service like phone.com that can quickly and efficiently send thousands of text messages. You can even outsource this process to a virtual assistant and only follow up on the leads that look like they have potential. If your virtual assistant is in an overseas time zone, be aware of the time difference and only send out messages at appropriate times.

As a test, I utilized this mass texting strategy with FSBOs and Zillow "Make Me Move" properties. Although I would not consider those groups of sellers motivated, I did get quite a large response since nearly everybody reads their text messages nowadays. You can use a phone.com number instead of your own cell phone for some privacy. Mass texting can be great for follow-up too. I know one company that does extremely well by following up with all their leads through multiple forms of communication, including text, email, and voicemail. All you really need is one or two good leads per day to get a substantial amount for the month and see some good opportunities.

Please note: Even though Google Voice allows you to send out text messages through their service, they will temporarily ban your phone number if you send out mass texts with their services, since it is a free tool. However, if you were to time-block just one hour a day where you sent out lots of text messages using a service like phone.com, and then combined that with door hangers, direct mail, or networking, you could be sure of getting leads.

Killer Retargeting Strategy

Retargeting is a more advanced strategy that you should absolutely utilize if you do a lot of online marketing. If your website gets a lot of visitors, you can add retargeting code to your website so visitors will see your ads on other websites after they leave. If you have ever looked at buying something on Amazon and notice that same product on an entirely different website a few days later, that is retargeting.

This strategy is fairly easy to implement. If you are not tech-savvy, you can easily pay someone on a website like Upwork to do retargeting for you. All the top-of-the-market investors I know use retargeting because they realize that the first time someone comes to a website they are not always ready to commit. However, by retargeting them you can "revive" many of these leads. Retargeting works best when you drive a ton of traffic to your website, either through pay-per-click or search engine optimization. If your website only has five visitors a month and you do retargeting, it won't be as powerful as if you had 5,000 people a month visiting your website.

The bottom line is, if you are not doing retargeting and you have a large online presence, then you are just leaving money on the table. I suggest reading a couple of case studies online to see the amazing potential of retargeting for any type of business.

The Truth About Social Media

Social Media Marketing is a great free resource that you should utilize in your off-market business. It is also constantly evolving, so if you become skilled at social media, you can target inefficiencies here and there to get your message out more effectively.

Most of the people I know that do very well on social media find private lenders, real estate agents, and partners for their deals. Social media such as Facebook or YouTube are great for testimonials from sellers, lenders, or real estate agents. You can generate a lot of buzz for your business on social media, and get interviewed by real estate podcasts and more. Some real estate professionals I know were even discovered by HGTV and other shows due to their social media marketing.

Motivated sellers (in my opinion) are typically not going on Facebook or Instagram to see who buys houses. However, with the growing number of users, it would be wise to implement some type of social media. The great thing about social media is that it is pretty much free. Moreover, there are tons of articles and resources online on how to optimize different parts of your social media.

My suggestion would be to find a "we buy houses" company in a different city and model their marketing on social media with your own twist. You always want to start with something that is proven, and then add on to it. Since social media is new and evolving, someone might crack the code on using it to find consistent off-market deals.

Invest In Car Graphics

Car graphics are an inexpensive way to generate consistent leads in your city. There are a couple of different ways to utilize this strategy. You can use just one or all of them to assist your business.

The first way is simple. All you have to do is order "we buy houses" car magnets that you can put on any vehicle you own. They are inexpensive and can get you in front of hundreds, if not thousands, of people every single day. I even know an investor who negotiated with her landlord to have a huge car sign saying "we buy houses" on a truck that she parked each day in the Walmart next to where she worked. As a result, she would get lots of leads. You can also park your car or truck with a large sign on the side of a busy road or intersection (as long as it's legal).

The second way is to wrap your contractors' cars in "we buy houses" paint or magnets, so when they are working on different houses, people will see them. I know many investors who do this and generate consistent leads from it. Often, since it is just a contractor van or pickup truck, the contractor will not mind having it on their car, and in some cases you can give them a referral fee if you buy a house from one of their ads.

A third way of utilizing this strategy is using a service like "Bandit Signs On Wheels" where they give you an affiliate number and you sign people up to put the ad on their car with a special extension so that you know where each lead came from. If you can get five, ten, 15, or even 100 people to sign up for this strategy, then you can have a whole fleet generating leads for you all around the city. With the popularity of Uber and other car services, this could be another way for people to have an additional income with their car. There is one investor I know that has about 80 people in his city driving around with their ad and phone number.

Overlooked Properties That Fall Out Of Contract

Every year I attend numerous marketing and real estate seminars. One interesting marketing strategy I heard came from an investor who contacts properties that are already under contract. Since the chances of a property falling out of contract are not as small as you think (he estimates them around 10-20 percent), the possibilities of finding deals this way is actually pretty good.

He contacts agents who have deals under contract and lets them know that he is a cash buyer looking for deals. He makes sure they know that if their deal falls out of contract, he might be interested in buying it. Since most agents give up after the property goes under contract, as a result of this strategy he gets tons of leads that almost no one even knows are available. These deals are technically listed on the MLS. Once they go under contract, it is safe to say almost nobody else is marketing to their agent about buying it as a backup offer. If you have been in real estate for a little while, you know how easy it is for a property to fall out of contract. Sometimes, that can make the seller super motivated and willing to drop their price.

You can be even more strategic about this tactic by only contacting properties under contract that are fixer upper or investment-style deals. Over the course of a couple of months, or even a year, I could guarantee that many of these investment deals will fall out of contract with the original buyer, thus leaving you with the opportunity to get the home even lower. One of the top investment companies I know does the majority of their deals by following up with agents and their marketing, as well as people who contacted them at one point. Be consistent!

Conclusion

I want to thank you for reading this book and I hope that you got a lot of value from it.

Like I mentioned, these are all of the strategies that myself and other top investors from around the country use to consistently make up to six and seven figures in the off market world. I have no doubt that if you implement these tactics you will dramatically increase your business and it will open you up to a world you may have not even knew existed.

If you received value from this book I would like to ask you a favor to leave me a helpful review on Amazon. Turn the next page to leave a review!

Thank you for your time and I wish you the best of luck in the off market world!

If you want to take the next step in the off market world, my book **OFF Market Real Estate Secrets** goes more in depth on everything you need to know in the off market world to be successful. Go ahead and check it out on Amazon today! http://amzn.to/2gi3S02

My YouTube channel also has additional marketing tips, cool videos, and more so please check it out and subscribe to stay up to date on all the action! http://bit.ly/2f5z6pl

Feel free to shoot me an email if you enjoyed the book or have any questions, I try to respond to every email I get and here is my personal email JRLeighton12@gmail.com

37704908R00029

Made in the USA
Columbia, SC
01 December 2018